W9-BCN-971

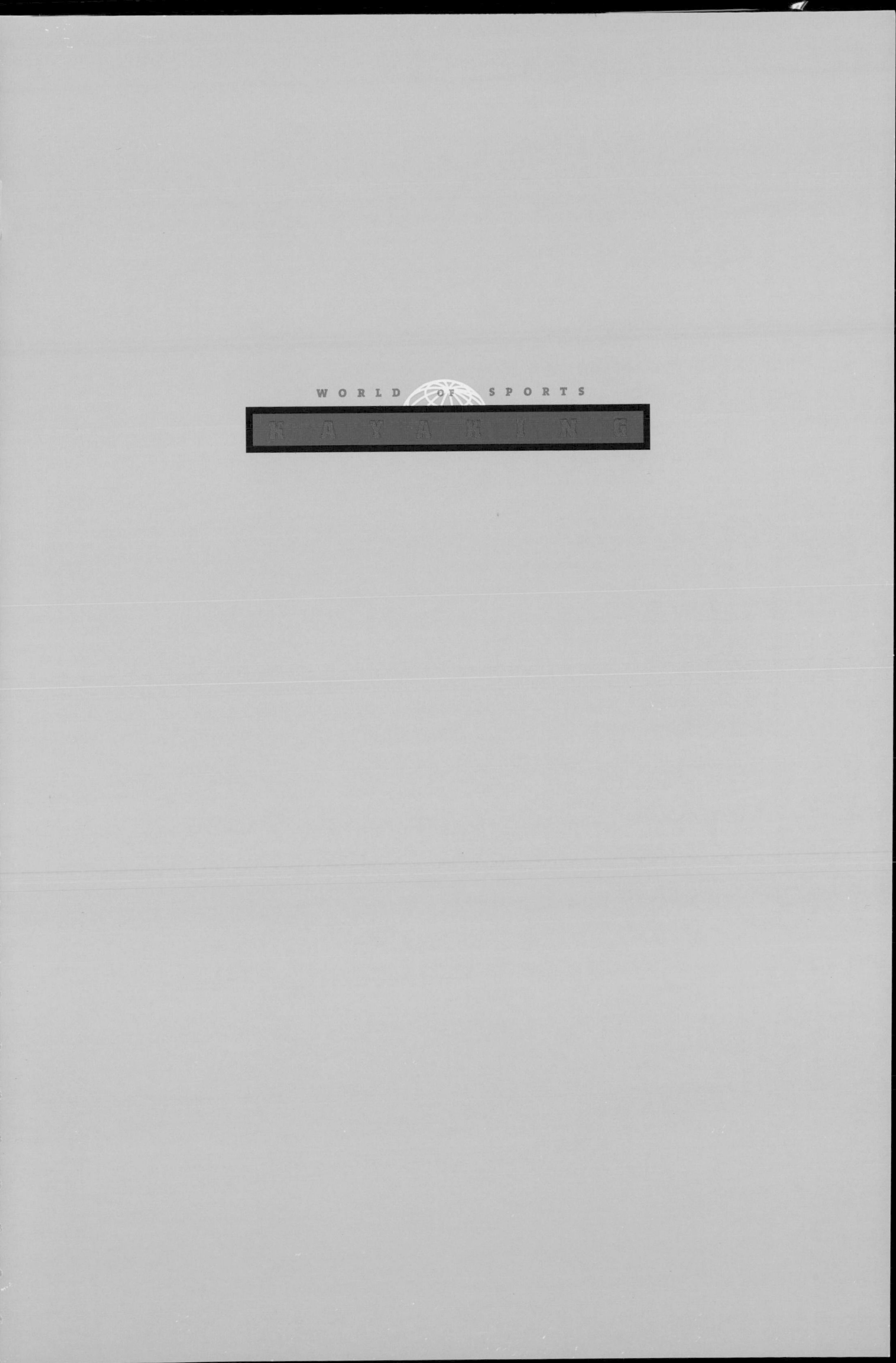
WORLD OF SPORTS
KAYAKING

Published by Smart Apple Media
123 South Broad Street, Mankato, Minnesota 56001

Photography: pages 7, 27, 28—CORBIS/Paul A. Sonders; page 11—CORBIS/Kevin R. Morris; page 13, 23—CORBIS/Joel W. Rodgers; page 14—CORBIS/Staffan Widstrand; page 15, 17—CORBIS/Karl Weatherly; page 16, 22, 30—CORBIS/ Jerome Prevost; page 19—CORBIS/Raymond Gehman

Design and Production by EvansDay Design

LIBRARY OF CONGRESS CATALOGING-IN-PUBLICATION DATA

Bach, Julie S., 1963–
Kayaking / by Julie Bach.
p. cm. — (World of sports)
Includes index.
Summary: Describes the history, equipment, and techniques involved in the sport of kayaking.
ISBN 1-887068-56-2
1. Kayaking—Juvenile literature. [1. Kayaking.] I. Title. II. Series: World of sports (Mankato, Minn.)
GV783.B32 2000
797.1'224—dc21 98-33681

First edition
9 8 7 6 5 4 3 2 1

JULIE BACH

Eventually, all things merge into one, and a river runs through it. The river was cut by the world's great flood and runs over rocks from the basement of time. On some of the rocks are timeless rain-drops. Under the rocks are the words, and some of the words are theirs. I am haunted by waters.

A River Runs Through It

by Norman Maclean

Running Rapids, Riding Waves

ON A SUNNY DAY in July, three **whitewater kayakers** stand on a cliff above Idaho's Big Mallard River, surveying the churning rapids beneath them. They enjoy the fast, thrilling, and sometimes dangerous rides down the swift-running stretches of river known as whitewater.

The rapids of the Big Mallard are rated Class IV on the International Scale of River Difficulty, a system that ranks rivers from Class I to Class VI. Class I rapids are suitable for a beginner. A Class IV stretch is considered difficult, and Class VI rapids are the most dangerous.

In 1931, Adolf Anderle, a Viennese kayaker, successfully boated the Salzachöfen Gorge on the Salzach River. His successful run of this dangerous river raised whitewater standards. Shortly afterward, kayaking organizations developed the International Scale of River Difficulty.

The kayakers on the Big Mallard see that they must stay to the left of a huge rock in the middle of the river to avoid a dangerous hole on the rock's right side. The hole is formed by swirling water, and it looks as if it could easily suck in a small boat. After passing the rock, the kayakers will face an abrupt, six-foot (1.8 m) drop. They will plunge through or

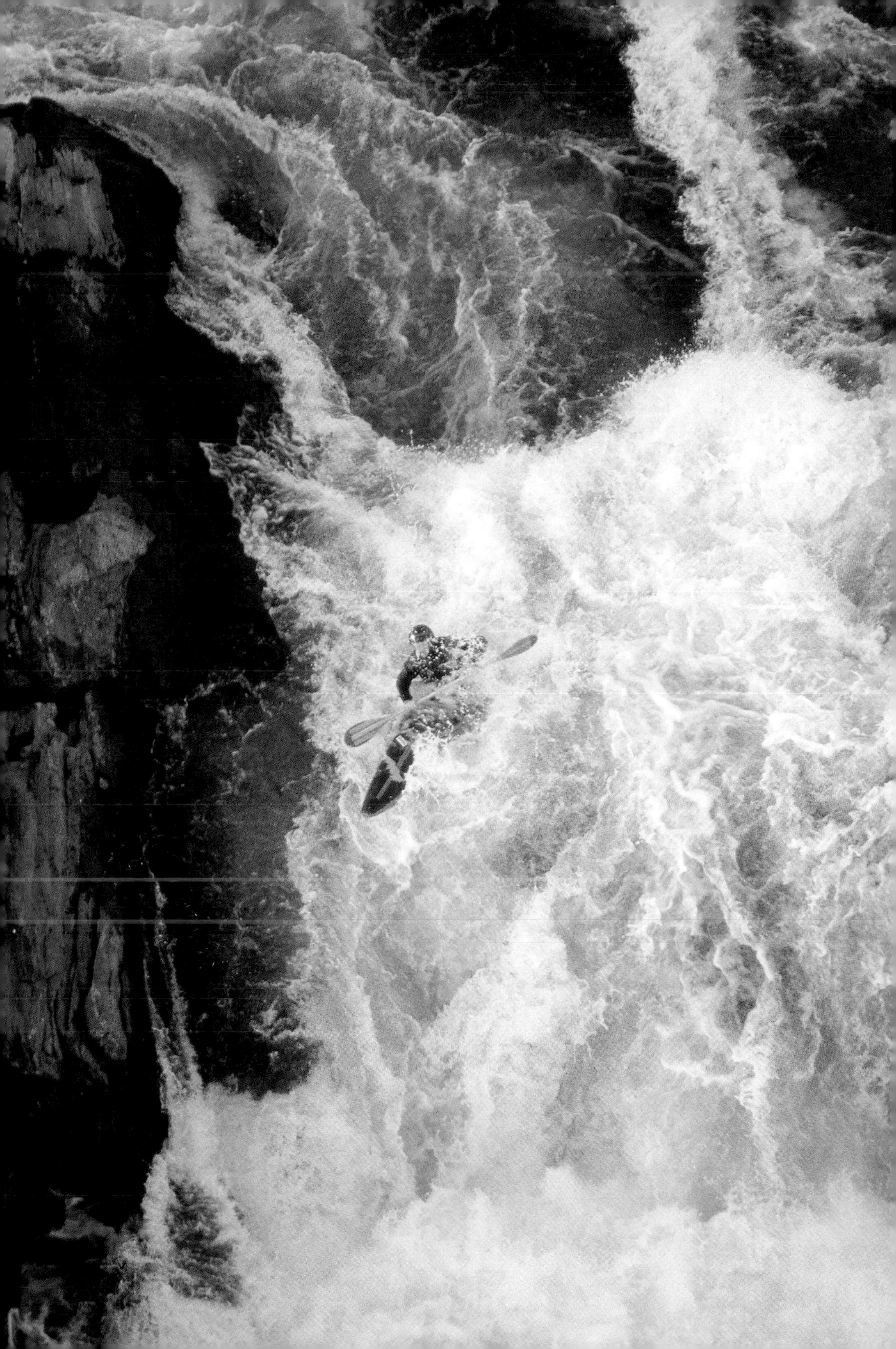

over a standing wave at the bottom of the drop before reaching calm water.

Hans Pawlata was the first European to roll his kayak. He successfully completed the roll on July 30, 1927, on the Weissensee River.

After visualizing it from above, the kayakers attack the challenge in the water. The first kayaker approaches the rapids right on target. She stays well to the left of the hole and plunges over the drop in a perfect line, her kayak sending up a spray of water that glistens in the sunshine. Then her bright yellow boat climbs the wave as water pours over her. Once through, she paddles over to calm water and waits for the others.

The second kayaker approaches the rapids in the same straight line. He, too, escapes the hole and plunges through

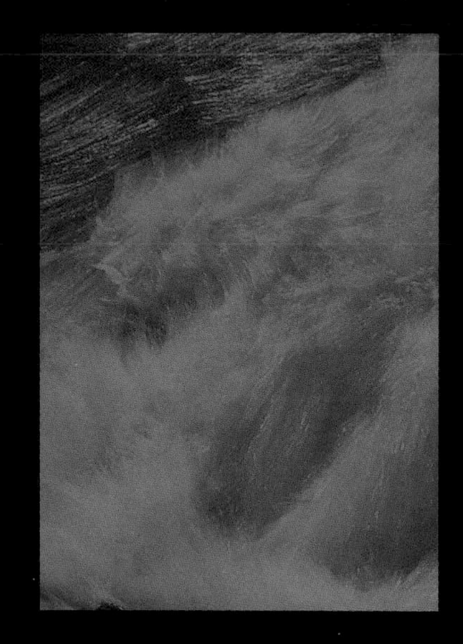

RIDING THROUGH CHURNING WHITEWATER IN A BOAT AS SMALL AND LIGHT AS A KAYAK IS A UNIQUE AND THRILLING EXPERIENCE.

whitewater kayakers *people who paddle a kayak on rivers, especially through rapids*

WHETHER SEEKING CALM WATER, WHITEWATER, OR WATERFALLS, KAYAKERS CAN CHOOSE FROM COUNTLESS RIVERS AROUND THE WORLD.

the wave at the bottom of the drop before paddling over to the pool of still water.

The final kayaker is not so fortunate. Just as he reaches the rock, his boat turns sideways. For a moment, his friends' hearts stop. It appears that the hole will suck him under. But he is an experienced kayaker. He deftly maneuvers his

paddle and skips away from the hole with a strong stroke, plunging recklessly down the drop. After punching through the wave, he paddles to the bank with water streaming down his smiling, sunburned face.

Hundreds of miles from the Big Mallard River, a lone female kayaker is having a very different kind of experience. She is a **sea kayaker**—an adventurer who journeys across the flat water of oceans or large lakes. Her sea kayak is bigger and more stable than the boats whitewater kayakers use to run rapids. She has packed food and camping gear in her boat.

The first kayak slalom race was held in 1934 in Switzerland on the Mühltraisen River.

On this chilly, overcast day, she is paddling among the islands of southeastern Alaska. She has been traveling for

A SEA KAYAKER HEADS OUT TO EXPERIENCE THE SIGHTS AND SOUNDS OF A TRIP ACROSS THE OCEAN'S BLUE EXPANSE.

sea kayaker *a person who paddles a kayak on oceans or large lakes*

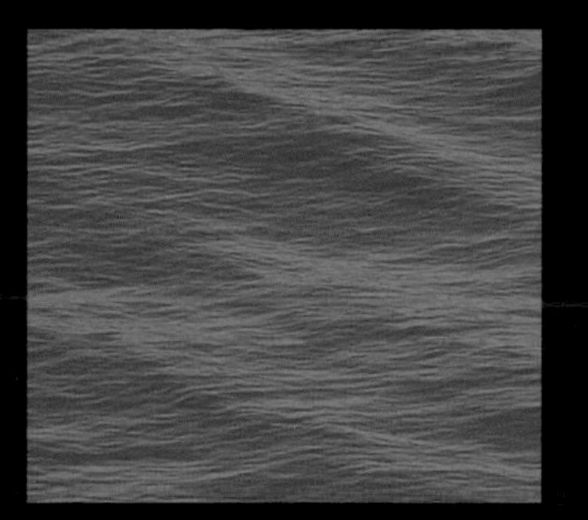

many days, camping each night in a different spot. Her goal is to reach Sitka, an island town farther south.

The winds are calm, and her surroundings are quiet as she paddles along. To her left are tall mountains that rise straight out of the ocean. Their slopes are green with pine trees, and their pinnacles are snow-capped. To her right is open water. In the distance, she sees a spray. Through binoculars, she sees a whale's back above the water. Eagles soar in the sky above her, looking for food. No boats pass; no planes fly overhead. She has waited for months for this trip, and it has proved worth the wait.

A GROUP OF KAYAKERS GATHER IN A CALM BAY TO RELAX FOR A FEW MOMENTS BEFORE RESUMING THEIR TRIP ALONG THE COAST OF WASHINGTON.

Out of the Arctic

PEOPLE HAVE MADE wooden boats for thousands of years. Most of these boats resembled today's canoes and skiffs—open to the wind and water. But in the arctic regions of Siberia, North America, and Greenland, native peoples came up with an ingenious design. They built long, narrow boats that were covered on top so the icy arctic waters could not get inside. Eventually, people started calling these boats kayaks.

At the 1996 Summer Games in Atlanta, Georgia, Dana Chladek overcame odds to become the only American whitewater kayaker to win a medal, taking silver in the women's slalom. She had been the lowest-ranked kayaker in the field and was next-to-last entering the second run.

The word kayak means "hunter's boat," and for the most part, that's what these boats were. Men used small kayaks to slip quietly within harpoon range of sea mammals such as seals, whales, and walruses. Larger kayaks were also sometimes used to transport people and belongings.

Inuits, Aleuts, and other groups of people modified kayaks for the part of the arctic in which they lived. The Aleuts, who lived in the

A GROUP OF CHILDREN IN GREENLAND LEARN HOW TO BUILD AND USE TRADITIONAL KAYAKS LIKE THEIR ANCESTORS ONCE DID.

southern part of the region, could use their fast-moving boats all year, because the oceans there never froze over. The Inuits, who lived much farther north, sometimes had to haul their kayaks on sleds across **ice floes**.

The people of these regions made kayaks out of driftwood and animal skins. They tied each boat together with **sinews** and used animal bladders filled with air to make the boats **buoyant**. They placed the bladders inside their boats at the very front and back. These air pockets made the boats virtually unsinkable.

A family might spend an entire winter building a new kayak or repairing an old one. No possession was more important. Without kayaks, people could not hunt for food.

When Russian explorers and traders ventured into these regions in the 18th century, they called the boats "baidarkas." Although they

In 1869, Major John Wesley Powell led an expedition through the Grand Canyon on the Colorado River. At that time, the river was considered unrunnable. However, Powell and his men completed the trip in three months despite meager supplies, lack of food, and even a wrecked boat. Many people consider his trip one of the greatest adventure stories of all time.

Gray clouds, blue icebergs, and silver water—a pair of kayakers take in the beauty of an Alaskan bay.

were impressed with the design, they did not try to build kayaks of their own.

In 1865, an Englishman named John MacGregor toured Europe in a kayak he built after seeing one on display. His boat, named *Rob Roy*, was the first kayak Europeans had ever seen.

Soon, people in France and Germany started boating down rivers for sport. These countries have many mountains, and the rivers that plunge out of the rocky slopes offer challenging rapids. At first, people ran the rivers in canoes. Then, in 1905, a German student built a collapsible kayak using an Inuit design. A tailor named Hans Klepper soon bought the

ice floes *large, floating islands of ice*

sinews *animal tissues that connect muscle to bone*

buoyant *able to float*

An olympic sport for more than 60 years, kayaking is exciting for both competitors and spectators.

patent from him and launched a business selling **foldboats**. Boaters could carry these wood and canvas boats in bundles and assemble them quickly on the shore of a river.

Germans fell in love with the new boats. They formed kayaking clubs and began to hold competitions. In 1936, **flatwater racing** became an Olympic sport at the Summer Games in Berlin, Germany.

Kayaks proved far superior to canoes for both river-running and flatwater paddling. They offered paddlers more control, maneuverability, and protection from the weather. In addition, one of the main advantages of a kayak is that the paddler can roll the boat over if it tips. Inuits and Aleuts developed the roll as a matter of survival in icy waters; Europeans learned to do it as an impressive stunt. This technique changed river-running forever. The roll meant that paddlers could attempt

foldboats *kayaks made of canvas and wood that fold into a small bundle*

flatwater racing *racing kayaks on the "flat" water of lakes or slow-moving rivers with no rapids*

capsized *overturned in the water*

fiberglass *a sturdy plastic reinforced with glass fibers*

more difficult rapids. If they **capsized**, they merely rolled themselves upright and continued down the river.

By the 1950s, kayak builders were using a new material called **fiberglass** that made kayaks more durable. The stronger material allowed paddlers to attempt rapids that were even more difficult. Stronger boats also meant that kayakers could compete in **slalom** races without fearing that their kayaks would break into pieces. At the Munich Summer Games in 1972, whitewater slalom racing was an Olympic event for the first time.

In 1975, Wick Walker, Tom McEwan, and Dan Schnurrenberger kayaked the Great Falls of the Potomac River—a stretch that had been feared for centuries. Since their successful run, all three kayakers have refused to reveal who was the first man over the Spout, the most deadly drop in the churning Great Falls rapids.

Many Inuits and Aleuts still hunt sea mammals for food. However, the cultures that invented the kayak now use modern boats equipped with outboard motors. The ancient art of building kayaks from driftwood, sinew, and animal skins has been all but lost.

The long, flat boats of sea kayaking enable kayakers to carry enough gear to take long trips across the ocean or the Great Lakes.

slalom *a type of racing in which competitors must pass through gates*

Boats and Equipment

TODAY, MANY KINDS of boats are made of fiberglass. What makes kayaks unique among small watercraft is their top cover, called the **deck**. The deck keeps everything inside the kayak dry, including the paddler's legs. Paddlers sit in a hole, or **cockpit**, in the center of the deck. Some kayaks have a two-person cockpit, but most are designed for a single paddler.

In 1977, Phil Coleman, Jim Snyder, and Mike Fentress became the first kayakers to descend Quarry Run, a tributary of the Cheat River in West Virginia. Coleman nearly died when his slalom kayak became embedded in the river's gravel bottom after a drop. Since that first run, paddlers who descend Quarry Run use inflatable boats that won't spear the river bottom.

Sea kayaks have a flat, stable **hull**. Whitewater kayaks have a rounded hull, which makes them a little tippier than sea kayaks, but also makes them easier to maneuver. Kayaks range in length from 9 to 21 feet (2.7 to 6.4 m). Most whitewater kayaks weigh less than 40 pounds (18 kg), making them easy to carry in and out of the water and allowing them to ride lightly over rapids. Sea kayaks are usually heavier—weighing up to 60 pounds (27 kg)—and sit lower in the water.

A paddler sits on a seat that hangs from the opening of the cockpit. In most boats, a woven strap supports the paddler's back. The seat includes a **hip brace** on each side, as well as **knee braces** and **foot braces**. The braces let the paddler "wear" the kayak, rather than just sit in it. For protection from drenching waves, the kayaker can snap a **spray-skirt** to the edge of the cockpit. The skirt surrounds the paddler's waist and keeps water out of the boat.

In 1994, Kent Wiggington became the first kayaker to run the rapids of the Tallulah River in northern Georgia. Wiggington wanted to demonstrate that the water was safe for recreation. His descent helped publicize a government decision to provide more recreational opportunities on the river by releasing water from an upriver dam.

Kayaks are designed to be buoyant and will float even if they are swamped by waves. A special kind of foam in the **bow** and the **stern** keeps them afloat even if they tip over. Many first-time kayakers are afraid of being trapped in their

deck *the cover or top of a kayak*

cockpit *a hole in the center of a kayak in which the paddler sits*

hull *the shell or main body of a kayak*

THE STRENGTH AND BUOYANCY OF KAYAKS ALLOW ADVENTURERS TO TACKLE EVEN THE MOST TURBULENT STRETCHES OF WATER.

FEW FORMS OF OUTDOOR RECREATION ARE AS ENTICING ON A HOT SUMMER DAY AS TAKING A DRENCHING ROLL IN A KAYAK.

boat if it overturns in the water. Fortunately, this is impossible. When an overturned paddler releases pressure against the braces and tugs aside the spray skirt, gravity helps the paddler slip out of the cockpit and swim away if necessary.

Most kayaks have **hatches** in which paddlers can store equipment. The hatches in sea kayaks are large enough to stow plenty of camping gear. Many sea kayaks also have **deck rigging** where paddlers put things they want to keep within easy reach, such as water bottles, maps, and binoculars.

Kayakers propel and control their boats with paddles. The paddles are made of wood, fiberglass, or aluminum. A paddle should be about one arm's length longer than the height of the person using it. The paddle can be two-headed or one-

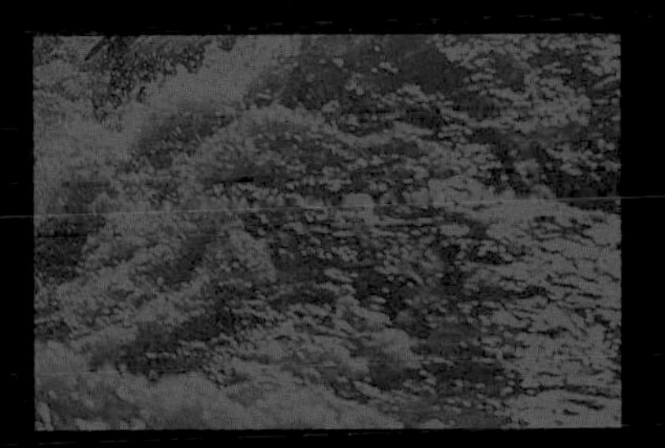

hip brace *a support connected to a kayaker's seat*

knee braces *supports inside a kayak for the paddler's knees*

foot braces *supports inside a kayak for the paddler's feet*

spray-skirt *a protective covering that attaches to the cockpit*

headed. A two-headed paddle has a flat blade on each end set at a right angle to the other for easier handling.

Life preservers, also called life jackets, are essential for all kayakers. They keep people afloat even in dangerous waters. In fact, a good life jacket will keep a person's nose and mouth out of the water even if the person is unconscious. In addition, whitewater kayakers use helmets to prevent head injuries from collisions with rocks or their own boats.

Whitewater kayaking and sea kayaking are both fun, easy to learn, and great forms of exercise. Many beginners start out by taking lessons in swimming pools. One of the techniques they learn is the roll—a basic safety maneuver. They twist their

Folding kayaks are still used by some paddlers for flatwater cruising and camping. These boats fold in half and are larger, roomier, and more stable than other types of kayaks.

bow *the front of a boat*

stern *the rear of a boat*

hatches *compartments to hold gear inside a kayak*

deck rigging *a mesh bag made of elastic bands that is attached to the hull of a boat*

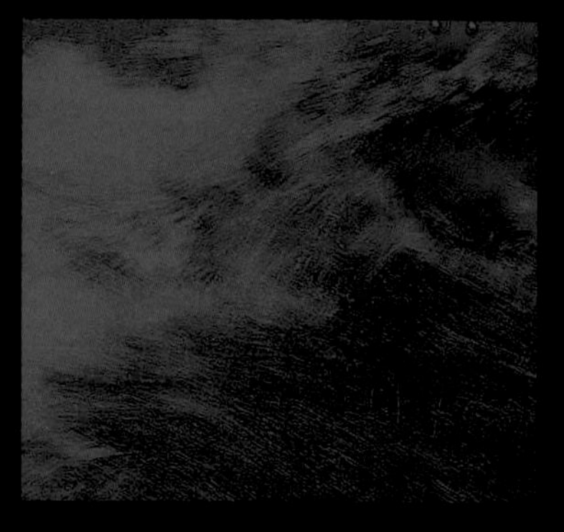

ORIGINALLY DEVELOPED AS A MEANS OF HUNTING SEALS AND WALRUSES, KAYAKING TODAY HAS BECOME A CAPTIVATING OLYMPIC SPORT.

upper body, using their paddles or arms to turn a capsized boat right side up.

Beginning whitewater paddlers usually test their skills on calm rivers with few rapids, taking on more challenging rivers as they gain experience. Sea kayakers begin by taking short trips in gentle waters. Many paddlers hire guides to take them on sea kayaking trips.

Gliding through a calm stretch of the Colorado River, a kayaker gets a spectacular perspective of the Grand Canyon.

Expeditions and Competitions

SEA KAYAKING IS also called ocean kayaking or bluewater kayak touring. It has been popular since the 1970s. Sea kayakers are more likely to go on expeditions than they are to enter races or run rapids. Casual sea kayakers might take a short, guided trip once or twice a year; others become intensely involved in the sport and venture out on lengthy, difficult expeditions. In a sense, many sea kayakers compete with themselves. They test their own endurance and abilities and continually try to improve them through experience.

On August 1, 1928, Captain Franz Romer was discovered asleep in his kayak in the harbor at St. Thomas in the Virgin Islands. He had paddled and sailed nearly 4,000 miles (6,436 km) from Lisbon, Portugal, surviving two hurricanes.

Expeditions can be as short as a weekend or as long as several months. Leigh Moorhouse, an accomplished sea paddler, completed a 2,100-mile (3,379 km) journey from Key Largo, Florida, to Eastport, Maine, in 1996 to raise money for breast cancer research.

Another top sea kayaker, Don Diamond, is the only person who has solo paddled across all five of the Great Lakes. Many people consider

Like skiers racing down icy hills, kayakers competing in the slalom weave in and out of gates while speeding down swift-running rivers.

him one of the world's strongest and most durable athletes in any sport.

Whitewater kayakers can compete in several racing events, the most popular of which is the slalom. Slalom courses are usually short stretches of moderately difficult rapids. Poles hang from ropes that stretch across the river, creating gates through which the racers must pass. If a racer touches a gate or pole, five penalty seconds are added to his finish time. Fifty seconds are added to a racer's time if he

KAYAKERS ATTEMPTING TO RUN RIVERS OF CLASS V OR VI DIFFICULTY MUST BE SKILLED WITH A PADDLE AND HAVE GREAT BALANCE.

misses a gate, goes through it backward or underwater, tips upside down while going through it, or intentionally moves a gate pole to get through. The paddler who completes the course in the shortest time wins the slalom.

Kara Weld is a four-time national champion in women's slalom. She joined the U.S. Canoe and Kayak Team in 1988 and won a bronze medal at the world championship competition in Slovenia in 1991.

Genevieve De Colmont became the first woman to pilot her own boat through the rapids of the Colorado River when she, her husband Bernard, and a friend kayaked the Green and Colorado Rivers in 1938. They proved that kayaks were better suited for running wild rivers than the heavy wooden boats favored by outdoor enthusiasts at the time.

Joe Jacobi, who won an Olympic gold medal in 1992, is another top slalom paddler. "I truly believe kayaking is a sport that anyone can do, but it's not necessarily for everybody," Jacobi said.

Another competitor describes slalom racing as "like playing golf when the tee and the green are in constant motion." Davey Hearn, a champion slalom racer and a member of the

U.S. kayaking team since 1977, explained the primary skills that a slalom racer needs. "You want to be fluid and fast," he said, "and miss the pole by maybe an inch or two."

Great paddling teams to beat in the 1996 Olympics were the Czech Republic, where kayaking has become a national pastime, Germany, and France. Kayakers from the Czech Republic took three gold medals; Italy, two; Germany, five; and Hungary, two. Norway, Slovakia, France, and Sweden each took one gold medal home.

Wildwater is another form of whitewater kayak competition. In wildwater racing, paddlers race for speed. There are no gates—just the boaters and the river. A more reckless kind of wildwater racing has become known as **hair boating**, in which kayakers compete on the most difficult rapids they can find. These competitions have more to do with

Roiling waters seem ready to overwhelm a whitewater kayaker as she powers through the waves.

wildwater *kayak racing for speed*

hair boating *kayak racing on extremely dangerous rapids*

whitewater rodeo *a type of kayaking event that involves stunts*

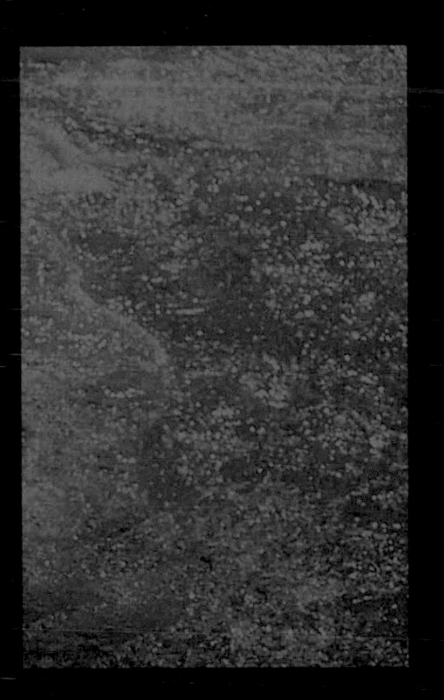

TRUE TO ITS NAME, WILDWATER KAYAKING IS ONE OF THE WILDEST FORMS OF COMPETITION, AS KAYAKERS RACE AT BREAKNECK SPEEDS.

survival than with racing, and they can be extremely dangerous.

Whitewater rodeo is a recent development in whitewater competition. During these events, kayakers in short, specially designed boats perform stunts in moderately difficult rapids. One of the most popular stunts performed by whitewater rodeo competitors is the "ender" or "pop-up." The paddler slides the kayak into a hole—a depression in the river where the water swirls in a circle—and tips the boat on its front end. The paddler is suspended horizontally in midair. From there, a kayaker might try a "retendo" or "cartwheel." In this stunt, the competitor actually makes the boat turn cartwheels from end to end as it's caught in the swirling water of the hole. Rodeo competitors are usually given 60 seconds to perform their routines and are judged

Using kayaks and dog sleds, four Spaniards formed the Circumpolar Expedition and traveled 8,680 miles (13,966 km) from Narsarsuaq, Greenland, to Valdez, Alaska. The expedition lasted from June 26, 1990, to March 25, 1993, making it the longest non-mechanized polar trek on record.

on technique, style, and variety. Younger people in particular enjoy this form of kayaking.

Risa Shimoda Callaway is one of the founders of the National Organization of Whitewater Rodeo. "I love competitiveness, with others or with myself," she said. "On each run, I have a goal and am psyched to achieve it."

But even the best kayakers cannot make a living by competing. Many of them earn money as kayaking instructors or guides. Some have written popular books that teach people how to safely enjoy the sport.

Many whitewater kayakers avoid formal competitions; instead, they are happy to compete with the rapids and simply enjoy the ride. There are so many different kinds of kayaking and so many places to paddle that kayakers can always find new adventures. Jim Snyder has been paddling whitewater for more than 30 years. "Kayaking is what you make it," Snyder said. "For me, that's very fun."

Between 1941 and 1943, 10 kayaks set out from Nazi-occupied Holland, attempting to cross the North Sea and reach freedom and safety in England. Only four of the double kayaks made it. The others were lost at sea.

Kayaking brings people into contact with nature. The small boats put them close to the water and take them to spectacular scenery. They experience the motion of the waves, the wind, and the currents. Kayakers can look at the environment from an intimate, personal perspective.

As a result, most kayakers are environmentalists who are careful to protect the environments they enter. They take all

THE 1996 SUMMER GAMES IN ATLANTA, GEORGIA, MARKED THE FIRST TIME THAT OLYMPIC KAYAKING COMPETITIONS WERE HELD ON A NATURAL RIVER—THE OCOEE RIVER.

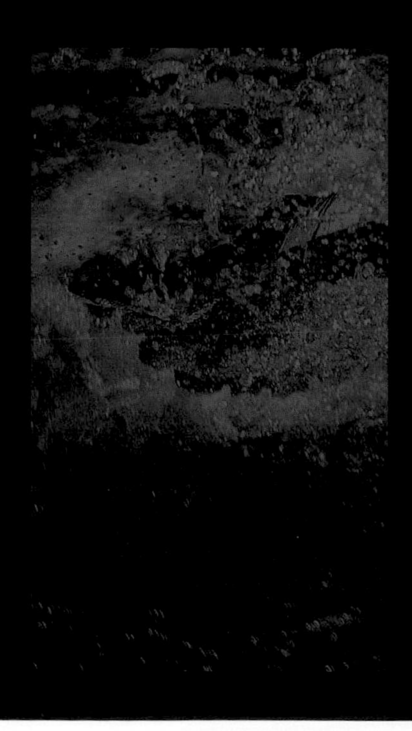

One of the reasons that many people love the sport of kayaking is that it brings them close to nature—and takes them far from society.

garbage with them and leave nothing behind. Some kayakers become environmental activists who fight to protect water quality and aquatic wildlife. They care about what happens to rivers, oceans, and lakes, in part because they want to paddle in these places. In fact, some kayakers would be happy to spend the rest of their lives on the water.

Sea kayaker Tina Godbert is one of them. "Once you're out there," she said, "you never, ever, want to come back."

INDEX